Rodale's High Health Cookbook Series

NO SALT NEEDED COOKBOOK

by the Editors of Rodale Books

Series Editorial Director:
Charles Gerras

Text Preparation:
Camille Cusumano
Carol Munson

Recipe Research and Editing:
Camille Bucci

Illustrations:
Jean Gardner

Art Director:
Karen A. Schell

Series Designer:
Jerry O'Brien

Copy Editing:
Jan Barckley

Cover Photography:
Carl Doney

Food Stylist:
Laura Hendry Reifsnyder

Rodale Press, Emmaus, Pennsylvania

Printed in the United States of America on recycled paper, containing a high percentage of de-inked fiber.

The recipes in this book have appeared in other Rodale publications.

Library of Congress Cataloging in Publication Data

Main entry under title:
No salt needed cookbook.

(Rodale's high health cookbook series; v. 3) Includes index.

1. Salt-free diet—Recipes. I. Rodale Books. II. Series.

RM237.8.N66 641.5′632 81-21192

ISBN 0-87857-393-3 hardcover AACR2

2 4 6 8 10 9 7 5 3 1 hardcover

Contents

No Salt—New Flavor Freedom 6

Appetizers, Relishes, Snacks, and Cereals 19

Soups 31

Main Dishes 39

Side Dishes 56

Salads and Dressings 73

Breads 85

Desserts 91

Index 96

No Salt—New Flavor Freedom

Anyone new to the idea of eating food without added salt is in for some happy surprises—a new world of flavors. Whatever the reason for cutting back on salt, people who stop using salt for a while are invariably amazed at how much better food tastes without it. After several weeks of experiencing the true flavors of food, no longer masked by salt, very few would consider a return to the old way.

If you are reluctant to give up salt all at once because you feel it might seriously affect your dining pleasure, phase it out of your diet gradually. Each week reduce by a quarter or a half the amount of salt you have been adding to your food. Soon you will begin to notice that the food served in restaurants seems salty to you. Commercially processed products will really be hard for you to swallow because of all the salt added at the factory. You will wonder how you ever got them down before! It will be a relief to get back to controlling the amount of salt in your food.

SODIUM AFFECTS HEALTH

The table salt (sodium chloride) we use to season our food contains about 40 percent sodium by weight. So, five grams (a teaspoon) of salt actually contains over two grams of sodium, which may be a threat to health when consumed in excess.

Sodium is an essential mineral, necessary in small amounts for good health. It has been estimated that the normal human requirement is about 500 milligrams daily. On the average, Americans consume about 5,000 milligrams a day—ten times the necessary amount!

Kidney failure, stroke and heart disease, edema (retention of body fluids), and migraine headaches are some of the health problems that can result from hypertension, an abnormality scientists link to excessive salt intake by susceptible people. Conversely, studies show that restriction of sodium can help to prevent high blood pressure or benefit those individuals who have already developed it.

Solving Baking Soda and Baking Powder Problems

For extremely restricted sodium diets, potassium bicarbonate, available at most drugstores, can be substituted for baking soda in baked goods. Baking soda contains 1,232 milligrams of sodium per teaspoon, and potassium bicarbonate contains none. Use about half as much potassium bicarbonate to replace the specified amount of regular baking soda.

Regular baking powder contains 350 milligrams of sodium per teaspoon, while low-sodium baking powder contains 1 milligram per teaspoon. You can find it in natural foods stores or pharmacies. If not, ask your druggist to make it up using this recipe:

Cornstarch	56.0 milligrams
Potassium Bicarbonate	79.5 milligrams
Potassium Bitartrate	112.25 milligrams
Tartaric Acid	15.0 milligrams

When substituting this baking powder, use only about half the amount of regular baking powder called for in the recipe.

Some doctors prescribe diets that limit sodium intake to 200 milligrams a day. Others go up to 1,000 milligrams. Diets at the low end require constant monitoring of the sodium content of all foods and beverages consumed because sodium occurs naturally in most of the things we eat and drink. It is in all foods of animal origin, such as fish, meat, poultry, eggs, and dairy products. It is also found in varying amounts in fruits and vegetables, and even in water. In general, fruits have little sodium; some vegetables, otherwise perfectly healthful, have a relatively large amount. Celery, artichokes, beets, spinach, and radishes are such foods and must be avoided in extreme low-sodium diets. For most people, who are merely out to cut out the extra sodium that comes from the saltshaker, these foods are fine.

Sodium Content without the Saltshaker

The following list will give you an idea of the natural sodium content in average servings of some foods *before* the saltshaker is used:

	Sodium Content (milligrams)
Barley (1 cup)	6
Carrots, sliced (1 cup)	51
Chicken Breast (½ pound)	145
Chicken Legs (½ pound)	195
Kidney Beans (1 cup)	4
Lima Beans (1 cup)	4
Milk (1 cup)	122
Rice, Brown (1 cup)	10
Salmon Steak, broiled and buttered	148
Spinach, cooked (1 cup)	90

FLAVORING WITHOUT SALTING

Those who stop using salt soon add new interest to foods. For example, lemon or lime slices or juices, as well as vinegar, work wonders in bringing out unsuspected flavors. Garlic and a wide variety of spices and herbs hold equally pleasant taste experiences. Buy herbs in small amounts and renew your stock frequently so you can use them at their peak of freshness and flavor. Among the other no-salt seasonings that can do wonders for your food are: meat glazes, pureed vegetables, fresh herbs, fruit sauces, and toasted nuts or seeds.

MEAT AND POULTRY

Marinating meat and poultry in herbed vinegar or lemon juice 12 to 24 hours before cooking acts not only as a flavoring, but as a tenderizer too. Doctors often specify the white meat of poultry for low-salt diets because the dark meat has a higher sodium content. Experienced cooks remove the skin from the meat before cooking because they know the exposed flesh will better absorb seasonings as it cooks. When frying meat or poultry, sear it over a high heat in its own fat, when possible,

Spiking Foods with Flavor

Asparagus: Sprinkle stalks and tips with fresh grated nutmeg before serving.
Chicken and fowl: Rub with garlic, sprinkle with lemon juice, and dust with paprika, sage, and thyme.
Cucumbers: Slice very thin and marinate in tarragon vinegar.
Eggplant baked with tomatoes: Add a bay leaf and oregano.
Eggs: Add a sprinkling of dill, oregano, or chopped chives.
Green beans: Season with nutmeg or savory.
Lamb chops and roasts: Rub with ginger, rosemary, or crushed black pepper.
Meats: Try a goulash or stew with bay leaves, sweet paprika, rosemary, or oregano.
Onions: Boil with cloves and thyme.
Tomatoes (fresh): Use basil, parsley, or thyme.
Veal (unsalted): Add chopped or powdered mint.
Seasoning with herbs: Instead of saltshakers on the table, provide attractive containers of oregano, basil, thyme, caraway seeds, sesame seeds, poppy seeds, or other herbs. You might also try allspice, chili powder, curry, ginger, home-prepared horseradish, lemon or lime juice, mustard seeds, peppermint, saffron, and tarragon.

Look Out! . . . High Sodium

Cutting down on salt may be especially difficult if you are used to eating foods preserved or processed with salt. Here is a list of some common ones. These foods are best avoided regardless of whether you are on a low-sodium diet.

Anchovies
Bacon
Bouillon Cubes
Cheese, Processed
Chips, Salted
Cold Cuts
Fish, Dried
Ham
Meat Extracts
Olives
Pickles
Sauerkraut
Sausage
Soups, Canned

because this causes the meat to release its juices, and it will cook in them. Brown the meat to a very dark brown to get the best flavor. You may also add some broth, lemon juice, or vinegar to flavor the meat and to prevent burning.

Degreased meat drippings provide a flavor bonus. After roasting any kind of meat or poultry, remove it from the pan and pour the drippings into a deep bowl. Put the bowl in the refrigerator or freezer until the fat solidifies on the surface and can be easily removed. Use these drippings to make gravy for the meat or to add extra flavor to stocks, soups, or sauces. A half cup contains about ten milligrams of sodium and only a few calories.

Sodium Content of Some Animal-Source Foods

Food	Portion Size	Milligrams
Bluefish	4 ounces	118
Chicken	4 ounces	70
Eggs	2 medium	108
Flounder	4 ounces	269
Ground Beef	4 ounces	76
Haddock	4 ounces	201
Halibut	4 ounces	152
Kidney	4 ounces	287
Lamb Leg	4 ounces	70
Liver	4 ounces	209
Lobster	4 ounces	238
Round Steak	4 ounces	80
Salmon	4 ounces	116
Shrimp	4 ounces	211
Sirloin Steak	4 ounces	64
Stew Meat	4 ounces	52
Turkey	4 ounces	148

Note: Food values, in general, are given for the form in which the foods are commonly eaten. Unless otherwise noted, most food values have been adapted from Agriculture Handbook No. 456, U.S. Department of Agriculture, 1975.

FISH

Fresh fish is an excellent source of protein, and most kinds of fish present no problem for those on a low-sodium diet. Shellfish is an exception. If your doctor has prescribed a very low sodium diet, avoid shrimp, scallops, lobster, and clams.

Fish that is marinated in lemon juice in the refrigerator for several hours is extra tender, moist, and tasty when cooked. Anise, fennel, basil, and thyme are other good seasonings that are especially compatible with fish.

DAIRY

Dairy products are often off limits for those on a very low sodium diet. However, egg and cheese dishes, carefully conceived, can provide a welcome and acceptable alternative to meat main courses. Omelets or frittatas can be made savory with garlic, onions, peppers, mushrooms, fresh herbs, and myriad combinations of low-sodium fillings. A non-salty cheese, such as natural Swiss, will make an excellent cheese pie that is both filling and elegant as a main course.

Sodium Content of Some Dairy Products

Food	Portion Size	Milligrams
Butter		
Salted	1 pat	49
Butter		
Unsalted	1 pat	0.5
Cheese		
American, Process Pasteurized	1 ounce	406
Cheddar	1 ounce	176
Cottage		
Creamed	4 ounces	457
Dry-curd	4 ounces	14
Mozzarella	1 ounce	106
Roquefort	1 ounce	513
Swiss	1 ounce	74

(continued on next page)

Sodium Content of Some Dairy Products–*continued*

Food	Portion Size	Milligrams
Cream		
Heavy	1 tablespoon	6
Light	1 tablespoon	5
Ice Cream		
Hard	1 cup	84
Soft	1 cup	109
Milk		
Low-fat	1 cup	150
Nonfat dry	¼ cup	161
Skim	1 cup	127
Whole	1 cup	122
Yogurt		
Whole-milk	1 cup	106

GRAINS AND LEGUMES

Grains and legumes are basic to the cuisines of many cultures around the world. Both have negligible amounts of sodium, *and* they provide good-quality nourishment. An added bonus is the discovery of the many individual flavors grains and legumes have to offer.

To further enhance the flavor of any grain, try cooking it in the broth from meat or vegetables, or even in fruit juices, instead of water. Marinate cooked legumes for zesty cold salads.

VEGETABLES

Fresh vegetables–delicate asparagus tips, dainty peas, florets of cauliflower, broccoli buds, tomato slices–offer a broad diversity of tastes in the form of low-sodium nourishment. Cucumbers, sliced carrots, grated cabbage, and chopped peppers are wonderful ingredients for raw vegetable salads, a healthy snack anytime. And salads need so little in the way of a dressing–just a sprinkling of vinegar and some herbs will do admirably. Several of the vegetables–celery, beets, spinach–may be a bit too high in sodium for highly restrictive diets.

One of the most nutritious ways to liven up vegetable salads is with fresh, crisp sprouts–low in sodium, low in calories.

If you want to cook the vegetables, it is easily done without increasing sodium intake. Stuff and bake the larger ones, such as eggplant and squash, with whole grains, herbs, wheat germ, onions, and garlic. Top them with herbed yogurt dressings. Serve them en casserole or in soups with grains or dried beans. Or simply saute or stir-fry some chopped vegetables with a little butter or sesame oil. Mix in some toasted seeds or nuts for extra flavor.

Sodium Content of Some Plant-Source Foods

Food	Portion Size	Milligrams
Apple	1 medium	1
Asparagus		
cooked	4 medium spears	1
Avocado	1 medium	9
Banana	1 medium	1
Beans		
Green Snap	½ cup	2.5
Kidney	½ cup	3
Beets	½ cup	43
Broccoli		
cooked	1 medium stalk	18
Brussels Sprouts	½ cup	8
Cabbage		
cooked	½ cup	20
Cantaloupe	½	33
Carrot		
raw	1 medium	34
Carrots		
cooked	½ cup	24
Cauliflower		
cooked	½ cup	5.5
Celery		
raw, chopped	½ cup	75
Corn	½ cup	trace
Cucumbers		
sliced	½ cup	3

(continued on next page)

Sodium Content of Some Plant-Source Foods—*continued*

Food	Portion Size	Milligrams
Eggplant cooked	½ cup	1
Grapefruit	½ cup	1
Grapes	10	2
Lettuce shredded	1 cup	5
Oatmeal salted	½ cup	262
Oatmeal unsalted	½ cup	1
Orange	1 medium	1
Peach	1 medium	1
Peanuts	10 jumbo	1
Peas cooked	½ cup	1
Pepper Sweet Red	1 medium	10
Pineapple diced	½ cup	1
Popcorn unsalted	1 cup	trace
Potato baked	1	6
Spinach cooked	½ cup	45
Spinach raw	½ cup	19
Sunflower Seeds	¼ cup	11
Tomato	1 medium	4
Walnuts	1 tablespoon	trace
Whole Wheat Flour	½ cup	4

SOUPS AND SAUCES

Soups and sauces benefit greatly from the addition of a well-seasoned—as opposed to well-salted—stock. Make a stock by long simmering of any combination of vegetables, herbs, and meat, poultry, or fish bones. Skim the liquid during the cooking, then strain it afterward and remove the fat. Stocks make not only tasty flavoring agents for soups and sauces, but excellent poaching liquids for vegetables, grains, meat, fish, and fowl. Savored by themselves, stocks are also great appetizers.

To strengthen the flavor in a meat stock, simmer it until much of the excess liquid evaporates. If you simmer a stock slowly for hours, you can reduce it to a residue of brown jell. This is called a meat glaze. It is a highly concentrated essence that can be used by the teaspoonful to season soups or sauces.

Creative blends of fruits, vegetables, meats, poultry, fish, grains, herbs, and spices also perk up soups and sauces. For example, try curry or minced parsley in a white sauce, or add barley to a tomato soup.

BREADS—YEAST AND QUICK

Homemade breads, muffins, biscuits, and pancakes add little salt to the diet, but those under strict sodium control can enjoy these foods made without salt, especially if they experiment with the many flavorful whole grain flours available in natural foods stores. What makes whole grain products so tasty even without salt is the presence of the grains' bran and germ.

Few things are more satisfying than a warm slice of whole wheat bread, an oat biscuit, or a bran muffin with a little unsalted butter, jam, or honey. When pancakes and crepes are served with meat or vegetables and a sauce, or topped with fruits, nuts, or seeds, the salt won't be missed. Just about any bread, muffin, biscuit, or pancake recipe can be enlivened by adding herbs, spices, pureed fruits, nuts, or dried fruits to the batter.

NUTS AND SEEDS

When served in their natural unsalted state, nuts and seeds are low in sodium and are delicious, nutritious energy foods that can be eaten as a snack, especially with fruit, or added to recipes to make many desserts, casseroles, and salads more exciting. They also add good taste and texture to grain, fish, and vegetable dishes.

Grind nuts in your blender and add them to baked goods or to sauces. Nut and seed butters are also delicious in sauces or added to fruit beverages. For extra flavor, roast nuts and seeds in a moderate (350°F) oven on a baking sheet for about five to ten minutes, or until they are lightly browned.

14 Common Seasonings and Their Uses

Allspice	**Breads**	Pumpkin Bread
	Meats	Beef
	Soups	Fruit
	Vegetables	Winter Squash
Basil	**Breads**	Herbed Biscuits, Yeast Breads
	Meats	Beef, Lamb, Meatballs, Stews
	Poultry	Chicken, Stuffing
	Soups	Minestrone, Pea, Potato, Spinach, Tomato, Vegetable
	Vegetables	Asparagus, Beets, Broccoli, Cabbage, Carrots, Celery, Cucumbers, Eggplant, Peas, Spinach, Tomatoes, Turnips, Winter Squash
Bay Leaf	**Meats**	Beef, Lamb, Pot Roast, Stews
	Poultry	Chicken Stew
	Soups	Chicken-Rice, Tomato, Vegetable
Cinnamon	**Breads**	Biscuits, Coffee Cakes, Fruit Breads, Muffins
	Meats	Beef Stew
	Soups	Fruit
	Vegetables	Beets, Carrots, Onions, Pumpkins, Sweet Potatoes, Tomatoes, Winter Squash
Cloves	**Breads**	Coffee Cakes, Fruit Breads
	Meats	Meatballs, Pork, Stews
	Soups	Onion, Stocks
	Vegetables	Beets, Carrots, Onions, Pumpkins, Sweet Potatoes, Tomatoes, Winter Squash
Curry	**Meats**	Beef, Fish, Lamb, Pork
	Poultry	Chicken, Stuffing
	Soups	Chicken, Consomme, Pea, Tomato, Vegetable
	Vegetables	Beets, Carrots, Parsnips, Sweet Potatoes, Turnips, Winter Squash
Dillweed	**Breads**	Biscuits, Dumplings, Yeast Breads
	Meats	Beef, Lamb
	Poultry	Chicken, Turkey
	Soups	Chicken and Noodle, Turkey

Dillweed—continued		
	Vegetables	Beets, Cucumbers, Green Beans, Potatoes, Tomatoes
Marjoram	**Breads**	Herbed Biscuits, Herbed Breads
	Meats	Beef, Meat Loaf, Pot Roast, Stews
	Poultry	Chicken, Stuffing, Turkey
	Soups	Creams, Onion, Potato
	Vegetables	Beans, Celery, Collard Greens, Onions, Peas, Potatoes, Turnip Greens
Nutmeg	**Breads**	Applesauce Bread, Banana Bread, Pumpkin Bread
	Meats	Meat Loaf, Swedish Meatballs
	Soups	Bean, Split Pea, Tomato
	Vegetables	Beans, Pumpkins, Tomatoes, Winter Squash
Oregano	**Meats**	Beef, Lamb, Meatballs, Meat Loaf, Roasts, Stews
	Soups	Bean, Minestrone, Tomato
	Vegetables	Broccoli, Cabbage, Eggplant, Lentils, Tomatoes
Paprika	**Breads**	Biscuits
	Meats	Hungarian Goulash
	Poultry	Chicken Paprikash, Garnish
	Soups	Bisques, Chowders, Creams, Pea
	Vegetables	Cauliflower, Potatoes
Rosemary	**Breads**	Herbed Biscuits, Herbed Breads
	Meats	Beef, Lamb, Pork, Roasts, Stews
	Poultry	Chicken, Pies, Stews, Stuffing, Turkey
	Soups	Chicken, Potato, Tomato
	Vegetables	Potatoes, Turnips
Sesame Seeds	**Breads**	Biscuits, Coffee Cakes, Rolls, Yeast Breads
	Poultry	Garnish, Stuffing
	Vegetables	Broccoli, Corn, Spinach, Summer Squash
Thyme	**Breads**	Corn Bread, Herbed Biscuits, Herbed Breads
	Meats	Beef, Lamb, Pork, Roasts, Stews
	Poultry	Chicken, Pies, Stews, Stuffing, Turkey
	Soups	Bisques, Chowders, Tomato, Vegetable
	Vegetables	Onions, Potatoes, Summer Squash

Sodium in the Pantry—Commercial Condiments

Food	Portion Size	Milligrams
Baking Powder	1 teaspoon	350
Baking Soda	1 teaspoon	1,123
Bouillon	1 cube	960
Catsup	1 tablespoon	156
Mustard, prepared	1 teaspoon	65
Olives, Green, pickled	5 large	463
Pickle, Dill	1 medium	928
Salad Dressing French	1 tablespoon	219
Salt	1 teaspoon	2,132
Soy Sauce	1 teaspoon	440
Steak Sauce	1 tablespoon	273
Tamari Soy Sauce	1 teaspoon	267

LOW-SODIUM OR NO-SALT CONDIMENTS

Vegetables and fruits (fresh and dried), plus an abundance of zesty herbs and spices are the basis for many flavorful condiments—concentrated forms of seasoning—that will help you forgo the saltshaker when eating eggs, vegetables, grains, and other foods. A quick, blender-made mayonnaise is handy to keep around for eggs and vegetables. Chutneys, mustard, catsup, and relishes are also good flavoring agents and are low-fat.

Check Your Water Supply for Sodium

People who must strictly monitor the sodium content of their food and beverages should know the sodium content of the local water supply. Sodium levels in water vary greatly from one area to another. If there are more than 30 milligrams of sodium per quart, it is advisable for low-sodium dieters to use some other water source for drinking and for cooking. Unfortunately, water softeners also add to the sodium problem.

APPETIZERS, RELISHES, SNACKS, AND CEREALS

Most appetizers are so irresistible that eating one cracker with dip leads to eating another and another. . . . So, if you're cutting back on your intake of salt, start by pruning away the ready-to-eat snacks that are filled and encrusted with salt.

Happily, all sorts of no-salt nibbles can be made in your own kitchen. Try roasting your own unsalted nuts and seeds, or rolling out your own salt-free, crunchy crackers. For a relish, enjoy crushed cranberries and oranges. Carrot sticks, celery sticks, cauliflower florets, broccoli spears, and green pepper strips teamed with an onion-yogurt dip are a welcome relief from a salty dip and chips.

In the following pages, you'll see many other suggestions for no-salt appetizers, relishes, snacks, and cereals, but don't let your imagination stop there. Vary the ingredients and you'll come up with still other delectable "appetite teasers."

Carrot Spread

- 1 carrot, cut into chunks
- ¼ cup unsalted peanuts
- 1 celery stalk (about 6 inches in length), cut up
- 1 hard-cooked egg, cut up
- 3 tablespoons unsalted mayonnaise (see Index)
- 1 teaspoon chopped onions

Place carrot chunks in a blender. Turn blender on and off until carrot pieces are shredded.

Add remaining ingredients and blend together. Machine will have to be stopped frequently and a rubber spatula used to stir ingredients. Blend until mixture is of a sour-cream consistency. Serve on bread or crackers.

Yields 1½ cups

Christmas Confetti Dip

⅔ cup yogurt

½ cup unsalted mayonnaise (see Index)

2 tablespoons chopped chives

2 tablespoons finely minced onions

2 tablespoons chopped green peppers

2 tablespoons finely snipped parsley

2 tablespoons chopped pimiento

⅛ teaspoon paprika

dash of cayenne pepper

Mix yogurt and mayonnaise in a small bowl. Add chives, onions, green peppers, parsley, pimiento, paprika, and cayenne. Mix together thoroughly. Taste and adjust seasoning.

Pour into a small serving bowl, cover, and place in refrigerator to blend flavors.

Yields about 1⅓ cups

Chop green peppers and fresh herbs such as chives, basil, and parsley, and store them in individual serving-size plastic bags. These freeze well, defrost quickly, and have more flavor than dried herbs.

Hummus

1 cup pureed chick-peas (also known as garbanzo beans) or ½ cup dried

½ cup tahini

1 clove garlic

3 tablespoons lemon juice

Garnish

dash of cayenne pepper

parsley

Soak ½ cup dried chick-peas in water overnight. Drain. Add fresh water and cook until tender (about 1½ hours). Add more water if necessary.

Puree chick-peas (save a few for garnish) in a blender, using a little of the cooking water, or mash them with a fork. Add tahini, garlic, and lemon juice. Process until smooth.

Spread on a flat platter and garnish with cayenne, parsley, and a few cooked chick-peas.

Serve with Indian puri or chapati.

Yields 1 cup

Mexican Garbanzo Beans

1 medium-size onion, coarsely chopped
2 cloves garlic, minced
1 stalk celery, coarsely chopped
1 green pepper, coarsely chopped
3 tablespoons oil
2 cups chopped tomatoes
1 cup cooked garbanzo beans
2 teaspoons dried oregano
1 teaspoon dried basil
½ teaspoon cumin
⅛ teaspoon chili powder

In a large skillet, saute onion, garlic, celery, and green pepper in oil until tender. Add tomatoes and saute briefly.

Combine sauteed vegetables with cooked garbanzo beans and seasonings and cook 30 minutes, or until thickened. Process in a blender until smooth.

Serve as a spread on bread or crackers.

Yields 3 cups

Apricot Chutney

- 2 cups dried apricots, cooked and chopped
- 2 to 4 tablespoons honey
- 1½ tablespoons vinegar
- 1 teaspoon minced ginger root or ½ teaspoon ginger powder
- ½ teaspoon coriander
- cayenne pepper to taste
- ½ cup raw cashews
- ½ cup raisins

Add all but the cashews and raisins to the apricots. The amount of spices, vinegar, and honey can be increased or decreased according to taste.

Add cashews and raisins and mix well. Serve with chicken curry or any cold meats.

Yields about 3 cups

Corn Relish

6 ears corn on cob, uncooked

1 green pepper, diced

1 red pepper, diced

2 medium-size onions, minced

1 1/3 tablespoons dry mustard

1/3 teaspoon dried turmeric

1/3 cup honey

1/2 cup vinegar

Remove corn from the cobs and combine with green and red peppers and onions in a medium-size bowl.

Combine remaining ingredients in a medium-size saucepan. Add corn mixture and simmer slowly 6 to 8 minutes.

Chill and serve.

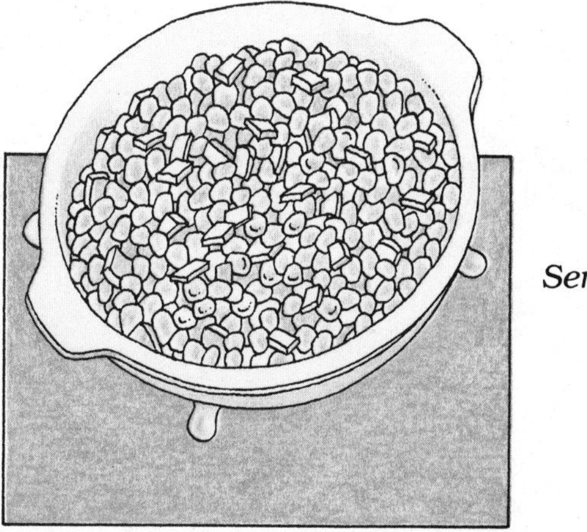

Serves 6

Nuts and Seeds

1 cup unblanched almonds
1 cup raw cashews
1 cup walnuts
1 cup Brazil nuts
1 cup sunflower seeds
1 cup pumpkin seeds
½ cup sesame seeds
2 cups raisins (optional)

All nuts should be raw and unsalted. Toss together and serve.

Yields about 6 cups

Nuts and seeds are rich sources of protein and minerals. They'll remain fresh for several months when stored in tightly covered containers in the refrigerator. For longer storage, keep them in the freezer.

Sesame Crisp Crackers

1 cup oat flour

¾ cup soy flour

¼ cup sesame seeds

¼ cup oil

½ cup water

Preheat oven to 350°F.

In a medium-size bowl, combine flours and seeds. Stir in oil and blend well. Add water and mix to pie-dough consistency.

Roll dough on floured surface to ⅛-inch thickness. Cut into squares or triangles, place on an ungreased baking sheet, and bake until crackers are crisp and golden brown (about 15 minutes).

Makes 3 to 4 dozen crackers

Oat flour is easy to make from rolled oats. Simply pulverize ¼ cup of oats in the blender. Empty the jar and repeat the process until you have the amount needed for a recipe.

Vermont Crackers

2 cups whole wheat flour
½ cup cornmeal
½ cup unsalted butter
¼ cup safflower oil
8 tablespoons milk
liquid lecithin for oiling pans

Preheat oven to 375°F.

Sift dry ingredients together in a medium-size bowl.

Cut butter into flour with a pastry blender. Add oil and milk and mix well to make a stiff dough.

Roll out as thin as possible. Cut with a cookie cutter or with a knife and place on an oiled baking sheet.

Crackers can be glazed with egg glaze and sprinkled with sesame seeds, poppy seeds, cheese, garlic powder, or any variation desired.

Bake 6 to 7 minutes. Turn crackers over with a spatula and bake a few more minutes until done.

Makes about 3 dozen crackers

Almond Crunch Cereal

3 cups rolled oats

1½ cups shredded coconut

½ cup wheat germ or soy grits

1 cup sunflower seeds

¼ cup sesame seeds

½ cup honey

¼ cup oil

½ cup cold water

1 cup slivered, blanched almonds

½ cup raisins (optional)

Preheat oven to 225°F.

In a large mixing bowl, combine rolled oats, coconut, wheat germ or soy grits, sunflower seeds, and sesame seeds. Toss ingredients together thoroughly.

Combine honey and oil in a separate bowl. Add to dry ingredients, stirring until well mixed. Add the cold water, a little at a time, mixing until crumbly.

Pour mixture into a large, heavy, shallow baking pan that has been lightly brushed with oil. Spread mixture evenly to edges of pan.

Place pan on middle rack of oven and bake 1½ hours, stirring every 15 minutes. Add almonds and continue to bake 30 minutes longer, or until mixture is thoroughly dry and light brown in color. Cereal should feel crisp to the touch.

Turn oven off and allow cereal to cool in oven. If raisins are to be added to cereal, do so at this point.

Remove cereal from oven, cool, and place in a tightly covered container. Store in a cool, dry place.

Serve plain or with fresh fruit.

Yields 8 cups

Hot Bran Cereal

5 cups milk

1 cup wheat, brown rice, rye, or a mixture of grains (toasted in a dry skillet and "cracked" in an electric blender)

¼ cup bran

honey or molasses to taste

raisins or other dried fruit (optional)

milk (optional)

Bring milk to a boil and stir in cracked grains and bran. Lower heat, cover pan, and simmer 5 to 10 minutes, or until cereal is as thick as desired. Sweeten with honey or molasses to taste. Add raisins or other dried fruit and more milk, if desired.

Serves 4

When cooked, cereal grains increase to several times their original amount—barley and millet increase to 4 times their size; all others increase to about 3 times their size. A good rule of thumb to use when planning individual breakfast servings is to allow ½ cup per person.

SOUPS

NO-SALT SOUPS

Homemade soups can be such splendid blends of herbs, spices, vegetables, meats, poultry, and fish that you'll never miss salt in them—unless you've been a regular consumer of commercially canned soups and dried soup mixes. The sodium content of these products is as much as 2,100 milligrams in a single cup!

As you make your own soups, feel free to experiment with various herbs and herb combinations. Try mint with pea soup; put rosemary or thyme into your chicken and rice soup. Use parsley to marry the flavors of two strong herbs, such as lovage and bay leaf. Parsley also has the power to mellow garlic.

For best flavor, add the herbs 20 to 30 minutes before cooking stops. That allows plenty of time for the volatile oils to be released into the soup, yet not so much time that the oils overheat and dissipate into the air.

Remember that soups benefit most when the use of herbs is light-handed. They should create a natural, understated background that enhances the flavors of the main ingredients, instead of overwhelming them.

Einlauf Soup

6 cups unsalted chicken stock

1 tablespoon cornstarch

2 tablespoons skim milk powder

½ cup water

6 eggs, beaten

chopped chives or parsley for garnish

Heat stock. Combine cornstarch and skim milk powder. Using a wire whisk, dissolve mixture in water and then add to beaten eggs. Mix well with whisk.

Beat egg mixture into hot stock, using whisk. Add chives or parsley and serve immediately. (Do not heat soup after adding egg mixture.)

Yields about 8 cups

Green Pea Soup

6 cups shelled green peas

1 medium-size onion, sliced

1 large potato, diced

1 large carrot, diced

few sprigs mint

4 cups water or unsalted chicken stock

pepper to taste

Cook vegetables and mint in water or stock until all are tender. Remove mint and put soup through a food mill. Add pepper, reheat if necessary, and serve.

Serves 6 to 8

Note: If you prefer a thicker soup, add a mixture of butter and flour until the desired consistency is reached. For a cream soup, substitute milk for half the stock, adding it after the soup has been put through the mill.

For maximum flavor and food value from vegetables, use the entire vegetable. Scrub, but don't peel potatoes, carrots, parsnips, and turnips. Save the tops of carrots, beets, turnips, and celery, as well as the stalks of broccoli and cauliflower. All make tasty additions to soups and stews.

Mushroom-Barley Soup

½ cup barley
4 cups water or unsalted stock
1 large bay leaf
2 carrots, sliced
1 small parsnip, sliced
½ cup coarsely chopped onions
½ teaspoon minced garlic
1 tablespoon oil or unsalted butter
½ pound mushrooms, sliced
1 teaspoon dried thyme
white pepper to taste
½ cup chopped parsley

In a 5-quart soup pot, simmer barley in water or stock with bay leaf until soft (about 1 hour). Add carrots and parsnip and simmer 15 minutes longer.

In a separate skillet, gently saute onions and garlic in oil or butter until wilted. Add mushrooms and thyme. Cook until soft. Then add onion-mushroom mixture and white pepper to the pot of barley. Bring to a boil, remove from heat, and let stand at least 5 minutes before serving. Sprinkle with parsley and ladle into preheated bowls.

Serves 4

Note: This soup reheats beautifully, but expect it to thicken. You can transform it into a stew by adding ½ cup lentils and sliced celery to the soup pot 45 minutes before the barley is done.

Norwegian Fruit Soup

- 1 cup large dried prunes
- 1 cup dried apricots
- ¾ cup raisins
- ½ cup dried currants
- 7 cups cold water
- 1 1-inch piece cinnamon stick
- 1 partially squeezed lemon
- 4 whole cloves
- 1 large apple, cored and chopped
- ½ orange, chopped (including pulp and skin)
- 4 slices unsweetened pineapple, cut into pieces, or ½ cup crushed
- 2 tablespoons honey
- ⅓ cup lemon juice
- 1½ tablespoons cornstarch
- 2 tablespoons cold water

In a large, heavy saucepan, combine dried fruits and 3 cups cold water. Add cinnamon stick and stud partially squeezed lemon (used for juice in recipe) with cloves and add to dried fruits in kettle. Place over medium heat, bring to a boil, and simmer 20 minutes.

Add apple, orange, and pineapple to cooked fruits. Stir in honey and lemon juice. Add remaining 4 cups cold water and continue to simmer 15 minutes longer.

Dissolve cornstarch in 2 tablespoons cold water, add to fruit mixture, and cook until slightly thickened, stirring constantly.

Yields about 8 cups

Note: This is a versatile dish and can be served hot or cold as a soup or as a dessert. Serve with yogurt.

Rosemary Minestrone

- ½ cup dried kidney beans or black beans
- 2 cups water or unsalted stock
- 1 medium-size onion, coarsely chopped
- 1 clove garlic, minced
- 1 4-inch rosemary branch tip
- 1 tablespoon olive oil
- 2 ripe tomatoes, peeled and chopped
- 2 or 3 celery leaves, chopped
- 1 small carrot, cut into chunks
- 1 scant cup chopped cabbage
- freshly ground pepper to taste
- 1 cup fresh green beans, broken into 1-inch pieces
- 1 tablespoon whole wheat macaroni
- grated Parmesan or Romano cheese for garnish

Wash and soak beans about 8 hours. Drain. Add water or stock, bring to a boil, and simmer, covered, 20 minutes.

Meanwhile, in a 3- or 4-quart saucepan, saute onion, garlic, and rosemary gently in oil about 5 minutes. Add tomatoes, celery leaves, carrot, cabbage, and some of the liquid from the beans. Bring to a gentle boil.

Add pepper and hot beans. Simmer 15 minutes. Add green beans and simmer 15 minutes more. Remove the rosemary—unless it's so tender you can't find it. Add hot water if needed. Five minutes before serving, add macaroni. Serve topped with grated Romano or Parmesan cheese.

Serves 4

Squash Bisque

1 small butternut squash, seeds removed

1 stalk celery

1 apple, cored

1 small potato

1 medium-size onion

1 carrot

¼ teaspoon crushed oregano

¼ teaspoon crushed rosemary

2 cups unsalted chicken stock

½ cup milk

Garnish

red pepper rings

herb sprigs

If you'll be pureeing soup in a blender, peel squash. If you'll be using a food mill, simply cut squash plus celery, apple, potato, onion, and carrot into chunks. Combine with oregano, rosemary, and stock in a 3-quart soup pot and cook until vegetables are tender. Run through food mill or puree in blender. Stir in milk. (If the soup is too thick at this point, add more milk or stock.)

Garnish and serve.

Yields 4 cups

Crush dried herbs and spices before using them. Crushing exposes many tiny surfaces and thus brings out the hidden essences.

Swedish Soybean Soup

2 cups dried soybeans
1 medium-size, meaty beef bone
3 quarts cold water
½ teaspoon paprika
1 cup chopped celery, with leaves
1 cup chopped onions
3 medium-size turnips, diced
¼ cup chopped parsley
⅛ teaspoon cayenne pepper
1 cup tomato puree
chopped parsley for garnish

Wash soybeans. Discard beans with imperfections. Add enough water to cover and place in refrigerator, covered, overnight.

The following day, place soybeans in a large, heavy soup pot. (Be sure to use a large enough pot and leave partially uncovered, so as to avoid soybeans cooking over. This can happen very easily.) Add beef bone and cold water. Place over medium heat and bring to a boil, uncovered, removing any foam from surface as it accumulates. Reduce heat, add paprika, cover partially, and simmer 3 hours, stirring occasionally.

Add celery, onions, turnips, parsley, cayenne, and tomato puree. Cover partially and simmer another hour, or until soybeans are tender. Continue to stir occasionally while cooking. Taste and correct seasoning. Garnish with parsley.

Yields about 3 quarts

MAIN DISHES

NO-SALT MAIN DISHES

Meat, poultry, fish, and grain main dishes take on new dimensions of flavor when prepared with savory seasonings and condiments in place of salt. That is because the freshness of garden vegetables and the zestiness of aromatic herbs bring out the best in these foods. Hardly anyone will reach for the saltshaker with such flavorful dishes as Acorn-Cabbage Bake on the bill of fare.

The recipes in this section also give you a choice of several exotic dishes to add to your menu. For a change from traditional cuisine, try the Bulgur Couscous recipe. Comprehensive enough to serve as a full meal, this dish is an unusual blend of lamb, fresh vegetables, and cracked wheat, seasoned with herbs and spices. What more could you ask from a low-sodium meal than such good-tasting nutrition?

Low-sodium meals without meat can also be tasty and satisfying main dishes. If you are a pasta fan, you will find Gnocchi a delectable diversion from a meat menu. The Fresh Herb Omelet is also a delicious way to add meatless variety and nutrition to a weekly menu.

Whether you prefer meat or vegetarian main dishes, you will agree that the recipes here all offer interesting choices for a salt-free diet.

Acorn-Cabbage Bake

2 large acorn squash

½ pound ground beef

2 tablespoons unsalted butter

1 medium-size onion, coarsely chopped

1 small apple, diced

2 cups shredded cabbage

2 tablespoons sunflower seeds

¼ teaspoon pepper

¼ teaspoon dried thyme

½ teaspoon dried sage

Preheat oven to 400°F.

Cut acorn squash in half lengthwise and scoop out seeds and fibers. Place squash in a baking pan, cut side down, and add ½ inch of water. Bake 20 minutes.

Meanwhile, saute ground beef in a skillet until browned. Drain off excess fat. Add butter, onion, apple, cabbage, and sunflower seeds and cook until vegetables are tender. Add seasonings and mix well.

Turn squash halves cut side up and fill centers with cabbage mixture. Return to baking pan and bake 30 minutes longer.

Serves 4

For those cutting down on salt gradually, tasty natural vegetables and herbs can be ground and put in a shaker for table use. Some that can be used in this way are: alfalfa, watercress, spinach, onions, celery, carrots, escarole, kale, and garlic.

Beef Liver a la Suisse

1 tablespoon cornmeal

2 tablespoons rye or whole wheat flour

1½ pounds beef liver, cut into strips 3 inches long and ½ inch thick

3 tablespoons oil

2 cups unsalted beef stock

½ teaspoon dried basil

⅛ teaspoon pepper

1 tablespoon cornstarch

2 tablespoons cold water

Combine cornmeal and flour and then coat liver thoroughly with mixture. Heat oil in a large skillet and saute liver about 15 minutes, or until tender and browned on all sides. Remove to a heated platter.

To the particles remaining in the pan, add stock, basil, and pepper. Bring to a boil, stirring to loosen any brown bits sticking to the pan.

Dissolve cornstarch in cold water and then add to the liquid in the pan, stirring constantly. Simmer sauce until clear and thickened. Pour sauce over liver and serve.

Serves 4 to 6

Beef Stew

3 pounds beef for stewing (chuck, round, brisket, or shin)

oil for browning

2 medium-size onions, coarsely chopped

4 carrots, cut in chunks

4 medium-size potatoes, cut in chunks (optional)

3 to 4 tablespoons potato flour or rye flour

½ cup cold water

chopped parsley for garnish

Cut meat into 1½-inch cubes, trimming off any fat. In a large skillet, brown meat in oil, using just a little at first and adding more as it is needed. Lift meat out and put in a 5-quart heavy-bottom pot.

Brown onions in same pan used for browning meat. The onions absorb the browned-meat juices, adding to the flavor of the stew. Add onions and juices to stew.

Put enough cool water in the pot to cover the meat, cover with a lid, and bring slowly to a boil. Then turn down heat and simmer 1 to 2 hours, or until meat is almost tender.

Add carrots and potatoes, if desired, and continue to simmer 30 minutes longer, or until vegetables and meat are tender.

Before serving, thicken stew by dissolving the flour in cold water, then adding a little of the hot juices from the pot carefully to the flour mixture, stirring constantly, until it is a smooth sauce. Pour sauce into stew, stirring carefully. Heat until flour is cooked (about 5 minutes). Garnish with chopped parsley.

Serves 6 to 8

Bran-Vegetable Meat Loaf

1 cup tomato juice

1 medium-size onion, quartered

1 clove garlic

1 stalk celery, cut into 1-inch pieces

1 carrot, cut into chunks

4 sprigs parsley

1 cup chopped broccoli or zucchini

1½ pounds ground beef

⅛ teaspoon pepper

1 teaspoon dried oregano

1 egg

¾ cup bran

Preheat oven to 350°F.

In an electric blender, combine tomato juice, onion, garlic, celery, carrot, parsley, and green vegetable. Process until completely pureed.

In a large bowl, mix remaining ingredients. Add pureed vegetables, combining well, and then place mixture in a 9 × 5 × 3-inch loaf pan. Bake 1 to 1¼ hours.

Serves 6

Bulgur Couscous

- ¾ cup chick-peas
- 2 pounds lamb, cut into 2-inch cubes
- 2 tablespoons oil
- 1 clove garlic, minced
- 3 medium-size onions, quartered
- 3 carrots, cut into 1-inch chunks
- ¼ teaspoon ginger
- ¼ teaspoon cumin
- ⅛ teaspoon cloves
- ½ teaspoon coriander
- 2 cups water (approximately)
- 2 cups bulgur (finely ground in electric blender)
- 2 small zucchini, cut into 1-inch slices and lightly steamed

Cook chick-peas according to preferred method. Drain and reserve liquid for future use in soup.

Brown lamb in oil, turning to sear all sides. Add garlic, onions, carrots, seasonings, and enough water to cover. Bring to a boil, lower heat, and simmer, covered, about 1 hour.

Meanwhile, using your hands, work about 1 cup water into bulgur, using enough water to moisten each grain. Put bulgur in cheesecloth-lined strainer that is small enough to fit into pot in which stew is cooking. Place strainer over the stew above the water level so bulgur will steam, not boil. Replace cover and cook 30 minutes. Remove strainer and turn

Bulgur Couscous—continued

out bulgur into a bowl. With your fingers, separate the grains and add enough water (about 1 cup) to again moisten all particles. Put bulgur back into strainer, replace over stew, and continue to steam another 15 minutes.

Remove bulgur and add cooked chick-peas and zucchini to the stew. Continue to cook just long enough to heat the chick-peas and zucchini.

Serve bulgur couscous immediately, topped with lamb stew.

Serves 6

Buckwheat Groat Patties

1 cup buckwheat groats

1 egg

2 cups boiling water

2 small onions, thinly sliced

½ pound mushrooms, chopped

1 teaspoon oil

1 tablespoon chopped parsley

2 eggs, slightly beaten

1 tablespoon chopped sunflower seeds

*I*n a heavy saucepan, combine groats with egg and cook until egg is completely absorbed. Add boiling water and simmer 15 to 20 minutes, or until water is absorbed.

While groats are cooking, saute onions and mushrooms in oil about 5 minutes. Mix sauteed vegetables with cooked groats. Add parsley, eggs, and sunflower seeds.

Form into patties or drop by the tablespoonful onto an oiled heated skillet. Saute both sides until nicely browned.

Makes 8 3-inch patties

Catfish Baked in Dill Sauce

1¼ pounds catfish, cleaned and skinned

2 tablespoons lemon juice

2 tablespoons unsalted butter

¾ cup yogurt

¼ cup milk

1 heaping tablespoon chopped parsley

2 teaspoons dried dillweed

Garnish

lemon

parsley

Preheat oven to 400°F.

Place fish in an ovenproof casserole. Sprinkle lemon juice over fish. Dot with butter. Bake, uncovered, 30 minutes.

Meanwhile, make sauce by combining yogurt, milk, parsley, and dillweed. After fish has baked 30 minutes, pour sauce over it and continue baking about 30 minutes longer, or until fish flakes. Garnish with lemon and parsley.

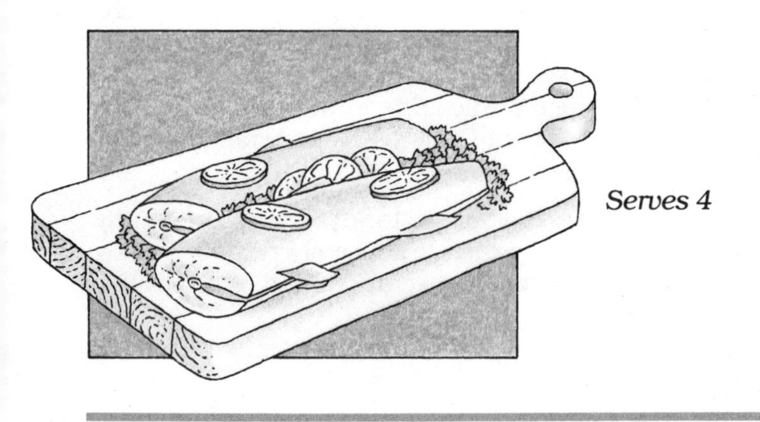

Serves 4

Chicken Paprika

- 2 chicken breasts, quartered
- 4 drumsticks
- 4 thighs
- ½ teaspoon turmeric
- 2 teaspoons paprika
- 2 tablespoons oil
- ½ cup chopped onions
- 2 to 3 cups unsalted chicken stock
- 1 tablespoon cornstarch
- 2 tablespoons cold water
- 1 cup yogurt
- 2 tablespoons chopped parsley
- fresh parsley sprigs for garnish

Wash chicken. Pat dry with paper towels. In a small bowl, combine turmeric and paprika and coat chicken with mixture.

In a Dutch oven or large skillet, brown chicken in oil. Stir in onions, saute briefly, and then add stock. Cover, bring to a boil, reduce heat, and simmer about 45 minutes. Remove lid and continue to simmer until stock is reduced by half. Chicken should be fork tender. Arrange chicken on a heated platter and keep warm.

Dissolve cornstarch in water and add to stock, stirring constantly. Cook until sauce is thickened. Add yogurt to sauce, stirring constantly. Stir in chopped parsley. Spoon sauce over chicken and garnish with additional parsley.

Serves 8

Fresh Herb Omelet

1 cup finely chopped spinach

½ cup coarsely chopped parsley

2 tablespoons snipped dillweed

2 tablespoons snipped chives

2 tablespoons snipped basil

¼ cup minced radishes

2 tablespoons minced onions

6 eggs, beaten

6 tablespoons water

Combine spinach, herbs, radishes, and onions. Combine eggs and water, and add to greens mixture.

Heat a cast-iron skillet or omelet pan to medium-high heat. Add just enough oil to pan to coat the bottom. Pour in omelet mixture, pushing cooked edges of omelet toward center of the pan with a metal spatula, and tipping the pan so the liquid will run to the outside rim and cook. When the omelet is almost set and the bottom is a golden brown color, lift up one side and fold it over the other side. Serve immediately.

Serves 4

Gnocchi

2 cups milk

½ cup yellow cornmeal

1½ teaspoons honey

1 cup grated natural Swiss cheese

2 tablespoons soft unsalted butter

2 eggs, beaten

2 cups tomato sauce (approximately)

Combine milk and cornmeal. Add honey and cook in a double boiler 30 minutes, or until cornmeal is soft and has absorbed most of the milk. Remove from heat and add ½ cup cheese, 1 tablespoon butter, and eggs, stirring each in to blend well. Spread at least ½ inch thick in an oiled, shallow ovenproof casserole. Cool and chill several hours or overnight.

Preheat oven to 375°F. Before baking, top with ½ cup cheese and 1 tablespoon butter. Bake 30 minutes. Cut into 1-inch squares and serve in tomato sauce.

Serves 6

In Northern Italy, *polenta*, or cornmeal mush, is a common replacement for bread. Cooked until very thick, the polenta is poured into a square pan. When it firms up, it is cut into squares, and the chunks of polenta are served with rabbit, fish, or fowl and topped with a sauce of stewed tomatoes, peppers, and onions.

Meatball Stew

1½ pounds lean ground beef

¾ cup whole-grain bread crumbs, moistened with water

1 tablespoon grated onions

1 egg

¼ teaspoon pepper

¼ teaspoon ground thyme

2 tablespoons oil

2 cups unsalted beef broth or chicken broth

5 medium-size potatoes, chunked

3 carrots, sliced

2 small onions, sliced

½ pound green beans, trimmed

2 tablespoons chopped parsley

Preheat oven to 350°F.

In a medium-size bowl, mix together beef, crumbs, grated onions, egg, pepper, and thyme until well blended. Form into 1-inch balls and brown in hot oil in a skillet. Remove from skillet with a slotted spoon.

In a 3-quart ovenproof casserole, gently mix meatballs, broth, potatoes, carrots, onions, green beans, and parsley. Cover and bake 45 minutes, or until vegetables are tender. Remove about ¾ cup of potato chunks, mash them, and return them to the casserole to thicken juices.

Serves 4

Scalloped Corn and Chicken

2 cups corn kernels (about 4 ears)

3 cups cubed, cooked chicken

2 tablespoons minced green peppers

2 tablespoons finely minced onions

1½ cups soft whole-grain bread crumbs

2 eggs, beaten

1 cup milk

2 tablespoons unsalted butter

Preheat oven to 375°F. Combine corn, chicken, green peppers, onions, and 1 cup of the bread crumbs. Add eggs and milk and turn into a greased 1½-quart ovenproof casserole.

Top with remaining bread crumbs, dot with butter, and bake about 25 minutes.

Serves 6

Steak and Kidney Pie

- 1 recipe Whole Wheat Flaky Pastry (see Index)
- 2 pounds beef for stewing
- 2 leeks, chopped
- 3 to 4 tablespoons oil
- 1 pound potatoes, peeled and cubed
- 1 beef kidney
- 4 teaspoons vinegar
- ¼ cup rye or whole wheat flour
- 1 cup water
- ½ teaspoon ginger
- ½ teaspoon allspice
- 1 egg yolk, beaten with 1 teaspoon water (optional)

Make pastry dough and set aside.

In a Dutch oven, brown beef and leeks in some of the oil. Add enough water to cover and cook, covered, until beef is tender (about 1 to 2 hours). Add potatoes for last 30 minutes of cooking.

Using kitchen shears, snip out fatty center of kidney. Cut kidney into ½-inch cubes, wash in water, and then combine with vinegar in a 1-quart bowl. Set aside 10 to 15 minutes. Drain on paper towels. Lightly saute kidney in remaining oil, just until it is no longer pink. Add to the cooked beef and potatoes.

Dissolve flour in water a little at a time and stir into stew. Simmer until thickened. Stir in ginger and allspice and turn into an ovenproof casserole.

Preheat oven to 400°F. Roll out pastry dough ¼ inch thick between sheets of wax paper. Wet rim of casserole and lay pastry on top, pressing it down over the rim all around to seal it. With a knife, slit the pastry in several places to allow steam to escape. Glaze top crust with egg yolk and water mixture, if desired.

Bake 30 minutes at 400°F, lower heat to 350°F, and continue to bake 30 minutes longer, or until crust is brown.

Serves 8

Turkey Divan

4 stalks broccoli or 8 stalks asparagus (about 1 pound)

2 tablespoons unsalted butter

4 tablespoons whole wheat flour

2 cups unsalted turkey stock

½ cup heavy cream, whipped, or ½ cup sour cream

pepper to taste

8 slices cooked turkey (about ¼ inch thick)

3 tablespoons grated Parmesan cheese

2 tablespoons slivered almonds

Steam broccoli or asparagus until just tender. Keep hot.

Melt butter in a saucepan. Add flour and blend thoroughly. Gradually add stock and cook, stirring constantly, until sauce is thick and smooth (about 10 minutes). Remove from heat.

Fold in whipped cream or sour cream. Season with pepper to taste.

Preheat oven to 350°F. Place broccoli or asparagus in a shallow ovenproof casserole. Pour half the sauce over it. Arrange sliced turkey over the sauce-covered vegetable. Add cheese to the remaining sauce and pour it over the turkey. Sprinkle with slivered almonds and bake until heated through and lightly browned. Serve immediately.

Serves 4

Zucchini Stuffed with Rice and Lamb

- 4 large zucchini (about 4 pounds)
- 2 medium-size onions, diced
- ¼ cup oil
- 1 pound ground lamb
- 1 cup cooked brown rice
- freshly ground pepper to taste
- ½ teaspoon mace
- ½ cup chopped parsley
- 2 tablespoons chopped mint
- 2½ cups cooked tomatoes
- 1 tablespoon cornstarch
- 1 tablespoon water

Halve zucchini and scoop out centers using an apple corer, taking care not to split them. Leave shells ½ inch thick. Dice zucchini taken from the centers.

Saute onions in oil until soft. Add lamb and saute until it is no longer pink. Add diced zucchini and cook 1 to 2 minutes. Then add rice and seasonings. Remove from heat and stir in parsley and mint. Stuff zucchini halves with mixture.

Place tomatoes and juice in the bottom of a heavy skillet, lay stuffed zucchini halves on top, cover skillet, and cook over medium heat 10 to 15 minutes, or until zucchini shells are tender but not too soft to hold the filling. Lift out the zucchini halves and keep them warm.

Dissolve cornstarch in water, add to tomato and juices in the skillet, and cook over low heat until thickened. Serve this sauce with the zucchini.

Serves 6

SIDE DISHES

NO-SALT SIDE DISHES

Of all the courses in a meal, side dishes are among the easiest to adapt to no-salt cooking. The fresh ingredients used in those dishes are so full of flavor! Occasionally, you might want to vary the tastes or intensify them with seasonings: chives, dillweed, tarragon, white pepper, curry, thyme, nutmeg.

When planning no-salt side dishes, consider the entire menu. Think of dishes that complement and harmonize with the main course, the appetizer, and the dessert. Use plain brown rice to relieve the assertiveness of a spicy curried chicken. Green peas add color interest to a meal of mashed potatoes and sliced turkey. Add appeal to plain beef patties by including the Asparagus with Pasta or the Hot Escarole and Potatoes Vinaigrette featured in this section.

Incidentally, one good way to think of side dishes is as an extension of the main dish. They complete its nutrition, texture, appearance, and, most of all, flavor.

Asparagus with Pasta

1 pound asparagus

1 medium-size onion, coarsely chopped

2 tablespoons oil

2 cups cooked drained tomatoes

½ teaspoon dried basil

¼ teaspoon pepper

½ pound whole wheat noodles

Wash asparagus and break off tough ends. Cut asparagus into 1-inch lengths.

In a large skillet, saute onion in oil until soft. Add tomatoes, basil, pepper, and asparagus. Simmer, partially covered, until asparagus is tender (about 20 minutes).

Meanwhile, cook noodles according to package directions. Serve asparagus and sauce over noodles.

Serves 4

Baked Onions and Bulgur
with Raisins

2 cups chopped onions

3 tablespoons unsalted butter

1 cup bulgur

½ teaspoon coriander

½ teaspoon cinnamon

2 cloves garlic, minced

3 cups unsalted beef stock, chicken stock, or vegetable stock

¼ cup raisins

⅛ teaspoon pepper

Preheat oven to 350°F.

Saute onions in butter a few minutes. Add bulgur, coriander, cinnamon, and garlic and saute several minutes longer.

Stir in stock, raisins, and pepper, turn into a buttered ovenproof casserole, and bake 30 minutes.

Serves 4 to 6

Onions

Spanish, yellow, and white onions are all cured or dried after harvesting, so their storage time is longer than that of the fresh members of their family, such as leeks and scallions. Cured onions will keep from 4 to 6 months if stored at temperatures of 35° to 40°F with no more than 60 to 70 percent humidity. You may also freeze onions. Unlike other vegetables, they need not be blanched. Just trim the ends, peel, and chop them before freezing.

Cauliflower and Peas
with Curry Cream Sauce

Sauce:

2 tablespoons unsalted butter

2 tablespoons whole wheat flour

1 teaspoon cumin

¾ teaspoon turmeric

½ teaspoon cardamom

1 cup milk

1 head cauliflower, cooked and separated into florets

2 cups cooked green peas

1 tablespoon chopped parsley

dash of paprika

Melt butter in a skillet or saucepan. Add flour and seasonings and blend into a *roux*. Gradually add milk and stir until sauce is smooth and thick.

Add cauliflower and peas and heat thoroughly. Top with parsley and paprika and serve immediately.

Serves 4 to 6

When cooking a whole cauliflower, place it stem down in a small amount of water and cover the pot tightly. This method allows the cauliflower to steam evenly and also preserves its white color.

Chilled Broccoli in Lemon Dressing

1 large bunch broccoli, separated into spears or chopped into bite-size pieces

¼ cup lemon juice

¼ cup oil

¼ teaspoon paprika

½ teaspoon honey

1 clove garlic, finely minced

1 tablespoon finely chopped onions

1 hard-cooked egg, chopped, for garnish

Steam broccoli until just tender. Drain well.

Combine all remaining ingredients except egg. Pour over broccoli and chill 3 to 4 hours to blend flavors.

Serve garnished with chopped egg.

Serves 4

When buying fresh broccoli, look for full dark green heads with tightly closed buds. A bluish or purple tint is OK, but avoid those with yellowish heads. This is a sign of age. Refrigerated, fresh broccoli will retain 90% of its vitamins for 24 hours. Before cooking the broccoli, trim off the woody base of the stalk. Then, cut the tough skin away from the stalk to insure quicker cooking.

Curried Broccoli and Carrots

2 medium-size onions, sliced

2 cloves garlic, minced

¼ cup oil

½ teaspoon turmeric

1 teaspoon coriander

1 teaspoon cumin

½ pound carrots (about 2 carrots)

1 pound broccoli (about ½ of large bunch)

⅛ teaspoon chili powder or crushed dried chili peppers

½ cup water, more if needed

In a large skillet, saute onions and garlic in oil a few minutes. Stir in turmeric, coriander, and cumin. Then add carrots, cover pan, lower heat, and steam 5 minutes.

Add broccoli, then chili powder, and finally add the water. Cover pan again and cook over low heat another 10 minutes, or until vegetables are tender but still firm.

Serves 4 to 6

Dilled Vegetables in a Rice Ring

2 cups cooked brown rice
¼ cup minced parsley
1 sweet red pepper, seeded and finely chopped (optional)
1 cup green beans, cut into 1-inch pieces
1 medium-size summer squash, quartered lengthwise and sliced
1 stalk celery with leaves, sliced
¾ cup water
3 tablespoons unsalted butter
1 tablespoon dried dillweed
pepper to taste

In a medium-size bowl, combine rice, parsley, and red pepper, if desired. Shape the rice mixture into a ring on a serving plate, or spoon the mixture into a ring mold and then unmold it onto a serving plate.

Combine green beans, squash, celery, and water in a saucepan. Cook, covered, until vegetables are tender (about 10 minutes). Drain well. (Save the liquid for soup.)

Cut butter into pieces and add it to the vegetables along with the dillweed and pepper. Stir to mix. Spoon vegetables into the center of the rice ring.

Serves 6

Green Beans
with Sunflower Seed Kernels

¼ cup unsalted butter
½ teaspoon dried marjoram
½ teaspoon dried basil
½ teaspoon dried chervil
pinch of dried savory
pinch of dried thyme
1 pound green beans
1 tablespoon chopped parsley
1 tablespoon chopped chives
1 clove garlic, minced
¼ cup sunflower seed kernels

Melt butter in a small saucepan and add marjoram, basil, chervil, savory, and thyme.

Wash beans, remove ends, and break into 1-inch pieces.

In a large skillet, add just enough water to cover the bottom of the pan and bring to a boil. Add parsley, chives, garlic, and beans and cook until beans are just tender-crisp.

Pour off excess water. Add herb butter and sunflower kernels. Stir to coat beans and toss over medium heat a few minutes, until well mixed.

Serves 6

Herb-Roasted Potatoes and Onions

- 6 large potatoes, quartered lengthwise
- 6 medium-size onions, quartered
- ⅓ cup oil
- pepper to taste
- 1 tablespoon dried parsley
- 1 teaspoon dried basil
- ½ teaspoon dried marjoram

Preheat oven to 375°F.

Put vegetables into a shallow roasting pan. Pour oil over vegetables. Sprinkle them with pepper, parsley, basil, and marjoram. Stir well to coat all sides with oil and seasonings.

Bake 1 hour, or until fork tender. Turn the vegetables occasionally, using a spatula, to loosen them from the bottom of the pan.

Serves 6

> Puree leftover vegetables or fruit in the blender; freeze in ice cube trays and remove only the quantity needed. Excellent for flavoring gelatin desserts or molded salads.

Hot Escarole and Potatoes Vinaigrette

4 tablespoons oil

2 medium-size potatoes, scrubbed

1 clove garlic, finely chopped

2 small onions, sliced and separated into rings

1 large head escarole

¼ teaspoon basil

pepper to taste

2 to 3 tablespoons cider vinegar

Heat oil in a large skillet over medium heat.

Slice potatoes ¼ inch thick and saute with garlic until potatoes are almost tender and golden on both sides.

Add onions, stir, reduce heat, cover pan, and cook slowly 5 minutes, or until potatoes are tender.

Separate escarole into leaves, discarding damaged ones. Break leaves into 1- to 2-inch pieces. Place in skillet with potatoes and onions, basil, and pepper to taste. Cook a few minutes, covered, only until escarole is wilted.

Remove from heat and toss with vinegar. Serve immediately.

Serves 6

Lentil, Rice and Prune Pilaf

- 1 cup brown rice
- 8 cups water
- 1 cup lentils
- 2 cups prunes
- 1 tablespoon honey
- 3 tablespoons lemon juice
- 1 stick cinnamon
- 3 cloves
- 3 tablespoons unsalted butter
- ¼ teaspoon dried mint
- ⅛ teaspoon tarragon

Cook rice in 2 cups water about 35 minutes, or until tender and all water is absorbed.

While rice is cooking, cook lentils in another saucepan in 4 cups water about 25 minutes, or until they are just tender but firm. Drain and combine with rice.

In a saucepan, combine prunes, 2 cups water, honey, lemon juice, cinnamon stick, and cloves. Cook 20 minutes. Drain prunes, reserving the liquid. Remove seeds and cut into quarters. Add to rice and lentil mixture and stir in butter, mint, and tarragon. Strain the reserved prune juice and add enough to moisten the dish. Simmer 3 to 5 minutes and serve.

Serves 6

Ratatouille

2 medium-size onions, sliced

1 clove garlic, minced

5 tablespoons olive oil

2 small zucchini (1 pound each), thinly sliced

2 small eggplants (about 1 pound each), peeled and cubed

2 green peppers, seeds removed and cut into 1-inch strips

5 tomatoes, peeled and quartered, or 2 cups cooked tomatoes, coarsely chopped

2 tablespoons snipped basil or ½ to 1 teaspoon dried basil leaves

2 tablespoons snipped parsley

¼ teaspoon freshly ground pepper

In a large heavy skillet, saute onions and garlic in 2 tablespoons olive oil 5 minutes.

Add zucchini, eggplants, and green peppers to skillet, adding more oil as needed. Stir gently, but thoroughly. Saute mixture 10 minutes.

Stir in tomatoes, basil, parsley, and pepper. Reduce heat, cover skillet tightly, and continue to simmer 15 minutes longer. Serve immediately.

Serves 8 to 10

Sesame Rice

½ cup chopped celery

½ cup chopped onions

½ cup chopped green peppers

½ cup chopped carrots

1 clove garlic, minced

3 tablespoons oil

¼ teaspoon each of paprika, sage, marjoram, and rosemary

1 cup brown rice

2 cups unsalted chicken stock or beef stock

2 tablespoons nutritional yeast

2 tablespoons toasted sesame seeds (toasted in a 200°F oven 20 minutes)

Saute all the vegetables in oil until onions are golden and celery is tender (about 10 minutes). Stir in herbs and rice.

Heat stock, then add to vegetable-rice mixture and bring to a boil. Stir in nutritional yeast and sesame seeds. Lower heat, cover, and simmer until all the liquid is absorbed and rice is tender (about 40 minutes).

Serves 4

Spanish Bulgur

2 tablespoons oil

1¼ cups bulgur

½ cup coarsely chopped onions

1 clove garlic, minced

½ cup diced green peppers

2 cups chopped tomatoes

¼ cup cooked dried beans

⅛ teaspoon pepper

1 teaspoon paprika

*H*eat oil in a heavy-bottom saucepan. Add bulgur and saute until golden.

Add remaining ingredients, cover, and bring to a boil. Reduce heat and simmer about 15 minutes.

Serves 4 to 6

Super Pilaf

2 tablespoons oil

1 medium-size onion, finely chopped

1 cup sliced mushrooms

1 cup barley

4 cups boiling water or unsalted stock

½ cup chopped dried apricots

⅓ cup unsalted chopped almonds

⅓ cup raisins

¼ teaspoon white pepper

1 teaspoon cinnamon

In a large heavy skillet or Dutch oven, heat oil and saute onion and mushrooms slowly until mushrooms are soft and onion is transparent. Remove to a covered dish.

In the same pan, saute the barley briefly (about 3 minutes). Do not allow it to brown or burn.

Add boiling water or stock to the barley, then add the mushroom-onion mixture and remaining ingredients. Do not stir.

Cover the pot and simmer over low heat until all the water is absorbed (about 1 hour).

Stir mixture carefully, place a tea towel over the pot (to absorb excess moisture), and replace the lid. Allow to stand 15 minutes before serving.

Serves 4 to 6

Sweet and Sour Red Cabbage

1 small head red cabbage

2 tart apples, cored and sliced

1 cup water

¼ teaspoon pepper

2 tablespoons unsalted butter

2 tablespoons cider vinegar

1 tablespoon honey

½ teaspoon caraway seeds

1 tablespoon cornstarch

¼ cup cold water

Wash cabbage, chop coarsely, and discard core.

In a large saucepan, combine cabbage, water, pepper, and butter. Cook, covered, until cabbage is tender-crisp (about 10 minutes). Add apples and cook 3 to 5 minutes, or until they are soft. Add vinegar, honey, and caraway seeds and stir.

Dissolve cornstarch in cold water and stir into cabbage-apple mixture. Simmer over low heat until sauce bubbles and thickens (about 1 minute).

Serves 6

Note: Green cabbage can be substituted for red.

When your menu calls for shredded or chopped cabbage, remember that 1 pound of raw cabbage will make 2 cups when cooked.

Turnips with Apples

1 pound turnips or rutabagas, cut into small pieces

3 tart apples, thinly sliced

pepper to taste

unsalted butter to taste

cinnamon for garnish

Steam turnips over boiling water until soft (about 20 minutes). Add apple slices and steam a few more minutes until soft. Remove from heat.

Mash together turnips and apples. Season with pepper and butter to taste. Sprinkle with cinnamon.

Serves 4

SALADS AND DRESSINGS

NO-SALT SALADS AND DRESSINGS

The saltshaker is one thing you don't need to bring out the good taste in a salad. With such appetizing ingredients as the white meat of chicken, pineapple chunks, and slivered almonds, you can orchestrate a blend of flavors that defy the use of salt. The Chicken Salad Oriental recipe, given in this section, does just that, and it is elaborate enough to be a main-course luncheon or dinner.

Salads often come to mind when you think of eating lightly. Salads can indeed be eaten as appetizers that furtively stimulate the appetite, but they can also serve as a full meal. The traditional salad of crisp greens is always a classic standby for a minor role, but the realm of salad possibilities is much broader. You can even transform leftovers into a delicious cold salad and accent them with any of the savory no-salt dressings given here.

An at-home "salad bar" is something the whole family can have fun with, and benefit from your homemade low-sodium condiments and dressings in the bargain. Vegetables, fruits, grains, and legumes can all serve well as the basis for an unusual salad. Just make small amounts of several of the salad recipes given in this section and let everyone find his or her favorite. Serve a choice of several dressings and enjoy the satisfaction that comes with providing your loved ones with a product free of the salt and additives of the commercial brands.

Chicken Salad Oriental

4 cups diced cooked chicken (white meat or a combination of white and dark)

1 cup drained, unsweetened pineapple chunks

⅔ cup water chestnuts, drained and thinly sliced

2 green onions, thinly sliced

½ cup chopped celery (optional)

½ cup yogurt

½ cup unsalted mayonnaise (see Index)

2 teaspoons lemon juice

1 tablespoon honey

1 teaspoon ginger

¼ teaspoon paprika

⅓ cup unsalted slivered almonds (toasted)

salad greens for garnish

*I*n a mixing bowl, combine chicken, pineapple, water chestnuts, green onions, and celery, if desired. Toss together lightly.

In a small mixing bowl, combine yogurt, mayonnaise, lemon juice, honey, ginger, and paprika. Blend together. Pour over chicken mixture and toss gently, but thoroughly. Chill in refrigerator, covered, at least 1 hour before serving.

Serve chicken salad on crisp greens, sprinkled with toasted almonds.

Serves 6

Cranberry Salad

1⅓ cups honey
1 cup water
4 cups cranberries, washed
2 tablespoons unflavored gelatin
¼ cup cold water
2 tablespoons lemon juice
1 cup diced celery
1 cup chopped unsalted walnuts

In a saucepan, combine honey and water. Place over medium heat and simmer about 5 minutes.

Add cranberries and cook slowly, without stirring, until all the skins pop open (about 5 minutes).

Soften gelatin in cold water and then dissolve in hot cranberry mixture. Add lemon juice and cool.

When mixture begins to thicken, fold in celery and walnuts. Transfer to a mold and chill until firm.

Unmold and serve with yogurt.

Serves 6 to 8

Fresh Mushroom Salad

1 pound mushrooms

5 tablespoons olive oil

2 tablespoons wine vinegar

¼ cup chopped parsley

1½ tablespoons chopped tarragon or 1 teaspoon dried

⅛ teaspoon freshly ground pepper

watercress for garnish

*R*inse mushrooms quickly, but thoroughly, in cold water. Remove the stems and reserve for another use.

Slice large mushroom caps crosswise about ¼ inch thick; small ones may be halved.

Place sliced mushrooms in a mixing bowl. Add olive oil, vinegar, parsley, tarragon, and pepper. Toss the salad well. Cover and allow to stand in the refrigerator 1 hour to blend flavors.

To serve, spoon salad into serving dish lined with fresh watercress.

Note: For variation, substitute fresh chopped dillweed instead of tarragon.

Serves 6

Summer Rice Salad

- 3 cups cooked brown rice
- 5 tablespoons olive oil
- 7 tablespoons wine vinegar
- 1 teaspoon snipped tarragon or ½ teaspoon dried
- ½ cup chopped green peppers
- ½ cup finely chopped celery
- ¼ cup chopped parsley
- ¼ cup finely chopped green onions
- 3 tablespoons chopped chives
- ½ cup diced cucumbers
- 3 tablespoons chopped pimiento

Garnish

- iceberg or romaine lettuce leaves
- hard-cooked eggs
- tomatoes

Place cooked brown rice in a large mixing bowl. Add olive oil, half of the vinegar, and tarragon to the rice. Toss together lightly. Cool at room temperature.

Add green peppers, celery, parsley, green onions, chives, and cucumbers to marinated rice. Add rest of vinegar, 1 tablespoon at a time. Reduce the amount of vinegar if a less tart salad is desired. Stir in pimiento.

Refrigerate rice salad, covered, until ready to serve; or, if desired, this salad may be served at room temperature.

Heap rice salad onto a serving dish, surround it with greens, and garnish with hard-cooked egg quarters and tomato slices or quarters.

Serves 6

Tomato-Bean Salad

3 cloves garlic, minced

1 teaspoon oregano

3 tablespoons olive oil

1 tablespoon wine vinegar

2 cups halved cherry tomatoes

2 cups cooked and chilled green beans

lettuce for garnish

In a small bowl, combine garlic, oregano, oil, and vinegar. Pour over tomatoes and beans and chill.

Serve on a bed of lettuce.

Serves 4 to 6

To keep the juice in the tomatoes when preparing sandwiches and salads, slice them with the core. Slice against the core to release the juice when making sauces.

Waldorf Salad

4 medium-size tart apples, cored and cubed (leave red skin on for color)

¼ cup chopped celery

¼ cup raisins

½ cup chopped unsalted walnuts

1 tablespoon lemon juice

2 tablespoons yogurt

2 tablespoons unsalted mayonnaise (see Index)

2 teaspoons honey

lettuce leaves for garnish

In a large bowl, combine apples, celery, raisins, and walnuts.

In a separate bowl, mix together lemon juice, yogurt, mayonnaise, and honey. Stir until well blended.

Add dressing to apple mixture, mix well, and serve on crisp lettuce leaves.

Serves 4 to 6

Blender Mayonnaise

1 egg or 2 egg yolks

2 tablespoons lemon juice or cider vinegar

½ teaspoon dry mustard

1⅓ cups oil

Combine egg or egg yolks, lemon juice or vinegar, and dry mustard in a blender. Blend together about 1 minute.

Gradually add oil, slowly but continuously, blending until all of the oil is incorporated. Stop blender and scrape down sides with a rubber scraper periodically.

Spoon mayonnaise into a glass container, cover, and store in refrigerator.

Yields about 1½ cups

Herb Dressing

½ cup oil

3 tablespoons wine vinegar

¼ teaspoon dried crushed thyme

¼ teaspoon dried crushed marjoram

1 teaspoon chopped tarragon or ¼ teaspoon dried crushed tarragon

1 tablespoon chopped basil or ½ teaspoon dried crushed basil

1 tablespoon snipped parsley

Combine all ingredients in a jar with a tight-fitting lid and shake vigorously. Allow to stand 15 minutes before serving.

Shake well before adding to crisp salad greens.

Yields ⅔ cup

Mock Green Goddess Dressing or Dip

1 cup unsalted mayonnaise (see Index)

½ cup yogurt

2 spring onions, cut in 1-inch pieces, including green parts

1 tablespoon tarragon vinegar

1½ teaspoons lemon juice

1 clove garlic, halved

½ cup watercress leaves

⅛ teaspoon cayenne pepper

Add ingredients to blender container in order given. Cover and process on high speed until onions are finely chopped and dressing is smooth in texture.

Pour into a small serving dish, cover, and refrigerate to allow flavors to blend.

Yields 1½ cups

Prepared Mustard

¼ cup dry mustard
¼ cup hot water
3 tablespoons white vinegar
⅛ teaspoon garlic powder
pinch of dried tarragon
¼ teaspoon molasses

Soak mustard in water and 1 tablespoon of the vinegar at least 2 hours.

Combine remaining vinegar, garlic, and tarragon in a separate bowl and let stand 30 minutes.

Strain tarragon from the second vinegar mixture and add liquid to the mustard mixture.

Stir in molasses.

Pour mustard into the top of a double boiler and set pan over simmering water. Cook until thickened (about 15 minutes). The mustard will thicken a bit more when chilled.

Remove from the heat and pour into a jar. Let cool, uncovered, and then put a lid on it and store in the refrigerator.

Yields ½ cup

Tomato Catsup

- 2½ quarts sliced tomatoes (15 to 17 tomatoes)
- 1 cup coarsely chopped onions
- 1 clove garlic, minced
- 2 stalks celery with tops, coarsely chopped
- 1 3-inch piece cinnamon stick
- 1 teaspoon whole cloves
- ½ teaspoon whole allspice
- ¼ teaspoon cayenne pepper
- 1 tablespoon dried basil
- 1 tablespoon dried oregano
- 1 cup vinegar
- 1 cup honey

Combine tomatoes, onions, garlic, celery, spices, and herbs in a 5-quart heavy-bottom pot and simmer, covered, 30 minutes. Press mixture through a sieve.

Add vinegar and honey to pureed mixture and simmer, uncovered, until mixture is reduced to half its volume. Stir frequently to prevent sticking.

Pour into clean, hot, sterilized jars, leaving a ¼-inch headspace. Adjust seals and process 5 minutes in a boiling water bath.

Yields 1 pint

BREADS

NO-SALT BREAD

Bread, rolls, muffins, and the like contain so many interesting, tasty ingredients, they certainly don't need salt to make them appealing. Seeds, nuts, raisins, honey, butter, and whole eggs—these are some of the fresh, natural ingredients that add something special to make your breads as irresistible as they can be.

Nothing evokes a greater sense of comfort and hospitality than the aroma and taste of a freshly baked loaf of bread. Even on a no-salt regimen, you can treat family and guests to this healthful pleasure. Just the sight of a thick slab of whole-grain bread lavished with melting butter and some honey will entice almost anybody away from undesirable sugary goodies.

You'll want to bake more often when you see how popular the home-baked product is. You can't purchase this kind of goodness from the supermarket, where salt, sugar, and preservatives are invariably part of the package.

You'll enjoy exploring other uses for the whole-grain and natural flours you keep around for baking. A few suggestions, such as the Rice and Soy Crepes recipe are given in this book. The crepes are handy, tasty salt-free wrappings for fruit and nuts or vegetables. Wholesome ingredients, high in flavor, don't need the added taste of salt.

Think of these recipes when you want to prepare a salt-free accompaniment to meals or a nutritious midday snack.

Bran Muffins

1 cup bran

1 cup whole wheat pastry flour

1 teaspoon cinnamon

2 tablespoons oil

1 cup milk

4 egg yolks, beaten

3 tablespoons honey or molasses

½ cup raisins, sunflower seeds, or unsalted nuts

4 egg whites

Preheat oven to 375°F.

In a medium-size bowl, combine bran, flour, and cinnamon.

In another bowl, combine oil, milk, egg yolks, and honey or molasses. Add to the dry ingredients. Add the raisins, seeds, or nuts or a combination of them—as you like.

Beat the egg whites until stiff and fold them into the batter. Bake in an oiled muffin pan or Pyrex custard cups 25 minutes.

Makes 8 muffins

Rice and Soy Crepes

4 eggs

2 tablespoons sesame oil

2 cups water

1 cup brown rice flour

½ cup soy flour

Combine all ingredients in an electric blender and process until batter is smooth. Let rest 2 hours to allow particles of flour to expand in liquid, resulting in a tender crepe.

Just before baking crepes, process again briefly to blend ingredients.

Heat an oiled crepe pan or a small, heavy skillet and drop batter by the heaping tablespoonful (about ¼ cup) into pan. Tilt pan to distribute batter evenly and cook about 2 minutes. Flip crepe over, using fingers, and brown on reverse side (about 1 minute). Remove crepe to heatproof plate and keep in warm oven until all the batter is used.

Makes 1 dozen 8-inch crepes

Sally Lunn

1 teaspoon honey
¼ cup lukewarm water
2 teaspoons dry yeast
1¾ cups milk, scalded
1 cup currants (optional)
½ cup unsalted butter
2 teaspoons cinnamon
1 cup chopped unsalted walnuts (optional)
3 cups whole wheat flour
4 egg yolks
½ cup honey
4 egg whites

Have eggs and flour at room temperature.

Combine 1 teaspoon honey with lukewarm water and sprinkle yeast on the surface. Set aside to soften. Combine scalded milk, currants, if desired, and butter.

Mix cinnamon and walnuts, if desired, into flour. Using an electric mixer, beat egg yolks briefly. Add ½ cup honey and beat until fluffy. Beat in yeast and milk mixtures. Gradually add the flour mixture and beat hard 3 minutes.

Beat egg whites until stiff. Fold one-fourth of the egg whites thoroughly into batter, then gently fold in remaining egg whites.

Gently turn batter into 2 well-buttered bread pans or 1 well-buttered 9-inch tube pan. Set pans or pan into a larger pan of warm water and let rise in a warm, draft-free place about 1 hour.

Carefully lift pans or pan out of water and into a cold oven. Turn oven to 400°F. After 15 minutes, turn oven to 325°F and continue to bake 25 to 30 minutes, or until a toothpick inserted in center of bread comes out clean. Remove pans or pan from oven and cool 5 minutes on wire rack. Gently loosen bread from sides of pan and then carefully turn out onto wire rack.

Makes 2 loaves or 1 9-inch cakelike bread

Spoon Bread

1½ cups milk
¾ cup cornmeal
3 egg yolks, lightly beaten
3 tablespoons oil
3 egg whites, stiffly beaten

Preheat oven to 375°F.

Scald milk. Stir in cornmeal and cook until thickened, stirring constantly. Add egg yolks and oil. Remove from heat and cool slightly.

Fold in egg whites and then pour into a well-greased 8-inch-square baking pan. Bake 35 to 40 minutes.

Serves 8

Whole Wheat Flaky Pastry

1 cup whole wheat pastry flour

1 cup brown rice flour

6 tablespoons unsalted butter

2 tablespoons oil

2 tablespoons ice water

Preheat oven to 400°F.

Sprinkle a 9-inch pie pan lightly with whole wheat flour.

Combine the flours in a bowl. Cut butter into flour with a pastry blender or knives. Add oil gradually, working it in with fingers. Then add ice water. Blend mixture briefly until water is evenly distributed.

Press into prepared pie pan, or roll out between well-floured sheets of wax paper and place in pie pan, making a high fluted edge around the outside.

If baking shell without filling, prick it well with a fork. Bake 10 to 12 minutes.

Makes 1 9-inch pie shell

If you're in the mood for pumpkin pie and you don't have pumpkin on hand, try substituting boiled, mashed rutabaga and marvel at the result.

DESSERTS

NO-SALT DESSERTS

Making a low-sodium dessert that tastes great is as easy as pie. No concern about the absence of salt here, since sweetness is the main characteristic of these dishes. It is encouraging for dieters to know that people who consume less salt often find that their craving for sugary foods also lessens. As a result, the natural sweetness of fruits—fresh and dried—assumes a more satisfying role in their diets.

When you bake your own desserts, you can decrease your dependence on the commercially manufactured refined sugar desserts (which generally contain added salt). You can also be more creative, using natural ingredients that enhance rather than hinder good health.

Everyone enjoys a taste of something sweet at the end of a meal. Why not make sure that the end of your meal is salt-free and nutritionally balanced, just as the other courses are? The Honey-Spice Cake recipe given here is one delicious way to do so. The Carob Chiffon *Pots* also incorporate nothing but nutritionally valuable, good-tasting ingredients. The recipes in this book transform the good nutrition of yogurt, buttermilk, eggs, whole-grain flours, and fresh fruit into the most satisfying of desserts. Best of all, no more guilt feelings as you enjoy snacks that can boast the natural goodness of Golden Apple Squares and the like at teatime.

Carob Chiffon Pots

1½ cups milk
2 envelopes unflavored gelatin
3 tablespoons carob powder
4 teaspoons honey
2 teaspoons vanilla
1 cup ice cubes (6 to 8)
¼ cup heavy cream, whipped
1 tablespoon finely chopped unsalted nuts

Put milk in a medium-size saucepan. Add gelatin, carob, and honey. Place over medium heat until gelatin is completely dissolved, stirring constantly. Remove from heat and add vanilla. Stir briskly with a wire whisk until well blended.

Pour mixture into a blender, add ice cubes, and process at medium speed until ice cubes have melted. Stir once or twice to be sure mixture is completely blended. Allow to stand about 5 minutes, until pudding starts to jell.

Spoon into *pots,* custard cups, or parfait glasses. Chill. When ready to serve, top with whipped cream and finely chopped nuts.

Serves 4 to 6

Golden Apple Squares

- ½ cup unsalted butter or oil
- ⅔ cup warmed honey
- 2 eggs
- 1 teaspoon vanilla
- ¼ cup buttermilk or yogurt
- ½ teaspoon soda
- 1¾ cups whole wheat pastry flour
- 1½ cups diced apples (unpeeled)
- ½ cup chopped unsalted pecans or walnuts

Preheat oven to 350°F and grease a 12 × 8-inch baking pan.

In a medium-size bowl, cream butter or oil and honey together. Then add eggs and beat until smooth. Add vanilla.

Combine buttermilk or yogurt with soda. Add to creamed mixture, then add flour and mix well.

Add apples and nuts. Pour into prepared pan and bake 35 minutes.

Makes 2 dozen 2-inch squares

Honey-Spice Cake

- 2/3 cup honey
- 6 large eggs, warmed in hot tap water
- 1 teaspoon vanilla
- 1 1/4 cups whole wheat pastry flour
- 1/2 teaspoon cinnamon
- 1/2 teaspoon ginger
- 1/2 cup unsalted butter, melted and warm

Preheat oven to 375°F.

Set mixing bowl in skillet that has water to the depth of about 1 inch in it. Heat water to simmering and keep this temperature throughout the mixing process.

Pour honey into the warmed bowl and add eggs and vanilla. Heat electric mixer beaters a few minutes in the oven. Beat egg mixture at medium speed until very thick and high (about 18 minutes). The eggs will form soft peaks when beaters are lifted.

Meanwhile, warm flour in oven, and then combine it with spices. Add flour mixture to egg mixture a little at a time, folding in gently with a rubber spatula. Add the melted butter (still warm) and fold in thoroughly.

Pour batter into buttered spring mold or 2 9-inch cake pans, and bake 35 minutes, or until cake is golden brown and the sides begin to pull away from the pan. Allow cake to cool in pan 20 minutes and then turn out onto wire rack.

Makes 1 high cake or 2 cake layers

Peach Upside Down Cake

¼ cup unsalted butter
¼ cup honey
1 teaspoon cinnamon
dash of nutmeg
2 cups sliced peaches
1 cup plus 1 tablespoon whole wheat flour
1 teaspoon soda
⅓ cup honey
¼ cup oil
½ cup buttermilk
1 tablespoon grated lemon rind
1 teaspoon vanilla
1 egg

Preheat oven to 350°F.

Melt butter in 8-inch-square baking pan. Add ¼ cup honey, cinnamon, and nutmeg and mix. Make sure mixture coats bottom of pan. Arrange peaches over butter mixture.

Combine flour and soda in a medium-size bowl. Set aside.

In a separate bowl, mix ⅓ cup honey, oil, buttermilk, lemon rind, and vanilla. Add to flour mixture, mix well, and then add egg. When completely blended, pour over peaches in pan. Bake 30 minutes.

Remove from pan immediately by inverting onto serving plate.

Serves 6 to 8

Index

A

Acorn-Cabbage Bake, 40
Almond Crunch Cereal, 29
Apricot Chutney, 24
Asparagus with Pasta, 57

B

Baked Onions and Bulgur with Raisins, 58
Beef Liver a la Suisse, 41
Beef Stew, 42
Blender Mayonnaise, 80
Bran Muffins, 86
Bran-Vegetable Meat Loaf, 43
breads, homemade, 15
broccoli, cooking of, 60

C

cabbage, 71
Carob Chiffon *Pots*, 92
Carrot Spread, 20
Catfish Baked in Dill Sauce, 47
cauliflower, cooking method for, 59
Cauliflower and Peas with Curry Cream Sauce, 59
cereal grains, 30
Chicken Paprika, 48
Chicken Salad Oriental, 74
Chilled Broccoli in Lemon Dressing, 60
Christmas Confetti Dip, 21
Corn Relish, 25
Cranberry Salad, 75
Curried Broccoli and Carrots, 61

D

Dilled Vegetables in a Rice Ring, 62

E

Einlauf Soup, 32

F

fish, marinating of, 11
flavoring
    marinating meat for, 8, 10
    spiking food with, 9
    vegetables and fruits as, 8, 64
food, sodium content of, 8–14
Fresh Herb Omelet, 49
Fresh Mushroom Salad, 76

G

Gnocchi, 50
Golden Apple Squares, 93
grains, enhancing flavor of, 12
Green Beans with Sunflower Seed Kernels, 63
Green Pea Soup, 33

H

health, effect of sodium on, 6–8
Herb Dressing, 81
Herb-Roasted Potatoes and Onions, 64
herbs
    crushing of, 37
    storing of, 21
    uses for (chart), 16–17
Honey-Spice Cake, 94
Hot Bran Cereal, 30
Hot Escarole and Potatoes Vinaigrette, 65
Hummus, 22

L

legumes, 12
Lentil, Rice and Prune Pilaf, 66

M

meat
    glaze, 15
    marinating for flavor, 8, 10
Meatball Stew, 51
Mexican Garbanzo Beans, 23
Mock Green Goddess Dressing or Dip, 82
Mushroom-Barley Soup, 34

N

Norwegian Fruit Soup, 35
nuts, storing of, 26
Nuts and Seeds, 26

O

oat flour, making of, 27
onions, storing of, 58

P

Peach Upside Down Cake, 95
Prepared Mustard, 83

R

Ratatouille, 67
Rice and Soy Crepes, 87
Rosemary Minestrone, 36

S

Sally Lunn, 88
salt, natural substitutes for, 40
Scalloped Corn and Chicken, 52
seasonings, uses for (chart), 16–17
seeds, storing of, 26
Sesame Crisp Crackers, 27
Sesame Rice, 68
sodium
    effect on health, 6–8
    in commercial condiments, 18
    content of foods, 8–14
    cutting back on, 6
    normal requirements of, 6
    in water supply, 18
soup, stocks, 14–15
Spanish Bulgur, 69
spices, uses for (chart), 16–17
Spoon Bread, 89
Squash Bisque, 37
Steak and Kidney Pie, 53
Summer Rice Salad, 77
Super Pilaf, 70
Swedish Soybean Soup, 38
Sweet and Sour Red Cabbage, 71

T

Tomato-Bean Salad, 78
Tomato Catsup, 84
tomatoes, slicing of, 78
Turkey Divan, 54
Turnips with Apples, 72

V

vegetables
    as low-sodium nourishment, 12–14
    maximum flavor from, 33

W

Waldorf Salad, 79
Whole Wheat Flaky Pastry, 90

Z

Zucchini Stuffed with Rice and Lamb, 55